Sri Guru

BASIC QUESTION ANSWERS FOR COMMUNICATION

Name : ____________________

Class : ____________________

Sec. : ____________________

Roll No. : ____________________

YouTube Channel: Sri Guru Academy

TITLE OF THE BOOK	:	**BASIC QUESTION ANSWERS FOR COMMUNICATION**
AUTHOR	:	**Thanga Durai** M.A., M.Phil.,
FIRST EDITION	:	2023
PAGES	:	110
PRICE	:	200/-
ISBN NUMBER	:	978-81-964961-2-8
PUBLISHER (Imprint)	:	**Sri Guru Publication** Madurai - 625 001. Cell: 75300 08201
E-MAIL ID	:	srigurupub@gmail.com
PRINTER	:	**Newsman Book Printers** Madurai - 625 020.

A question word is a word that is used to ask a question.

Wh - question starts with a **wh** word such as who, what, when, where, why, whose, how, which, whom etc. These words are called **Wh** words because most of them start with 'Wh'. It's main purpose is to seek content information relating to persons, time, place, facts, things, reason, manner etc.

What :

It is used to know about something.
e.g. What are they doing?

When :

It is used to know about time of an event or action.
e.g. When did it happen?

Where :

It is used to know about place or position.
e.g. Where are you going?

Who :

It is used to know about a person (subject) who did the action.
e.g. Who did this?

Why :

It is used to know about reason or cause.
e.g. Why are they laughing?

Which :

It is used to know about choices.
e.g. Which one do you like?

Whose :

It is used to know about the ownership or the possession.
e.g. Whose pen is this?

Whom :

It is used to know about a person.

Whom did you see?

How :

It is used to know about a process, condition, quality or manner.

e.g. How is the weather today?

Should :

To ask questions

e.g. Should we turn left at this street?

Would :

To make a polite request.

e.g. Would you like any tea?

Could :

To make a polite request.

e.g. Could you please move this box?

Can :

We use can to ask for permission to do something.

e.g. Can I ask a question, please?

Do, Did, Does :

Questions with do, did and does, as the first word usually elicit

'yes' or 'no' answer.

e.g. Do you like it?, No, I don't like it.

Did you finish it?, yes, I finished.

- Does she speak English? Yes, she speaks English.

- **What is your name?**
  My name is Kevin

- **What is your age?**
  My age is 16

- **How old are you?**
  I am 21 years old

- **Where do you live?**
  I live in Delhi

- **Whom do you live with?**
  I live with my family

- **Where do you come from?**
  I come from Madurai

- **Which is your native place?**
  My native place is Madurai

- **What is your father's name?**
  My father's name is Anand

- **What is your father?**
  He is a teacher

- **What is your mother's name?**
  My mother's name is Aruna

- **What is your mother?**
  She is a homemaker

- **What is your hobby?**
  My hobby is reading books

- **Where do you study?**
  I study in Mumbai

- **Who is he?**
  He is my friend

- **What is his name?**
  His name is Arun

- **Who is she?**
  She is my sister

- **What's her name?**
  Her name is Rani

- **Who are you?**
  I am a student

- **What are you doing?**
  I am studying seventh standard

- **Who are they?**
  They are my friends

- **Where is my book?**
  It is on the table

- **What is she doing?**
  She is cooking

- **When do you wake up?**
  I wake up at 6 a.m.

- **When is your birthday?**
  My birthday is on 26 January

- **When will you go?**
  I will go tonight

- **How do you go to school?**
  I go to school by bus

- **When will you come?**
  I will come tomorrow

- **What are you doing?**
  I am writing homework

- **What is he doing?**
  He is studying

- **Where is your sister?**
  She is watching T.V.

- **What did you eat?**
  I ate dosa

- **Where is he?**
  I don't know

- **Who is your friend?**
  Rahul is my friend

- **What is your mother doing?**
  She is washing the clothes

- **What are they doing?**
  They are writing homework

- **Where is your mother?**
  She is in the kitchen

- **Why are you late?**
  I missed the bus

- **Are you vegetarian?**
  Yes, I am vegetarian

- **How are you?**
  I am fine

- **How is your mother?**
  She is fine

- **Where is my phone?**
  It is on the table

- **Where are you going?**
  I am going to school

- **When will you return?**
  I will return tomorrow

- **When is your birthday?**
  My birthday is on 26th July

- **Do you know her?**
  Yes, I know her

- **Where does she live?**
  She lives in Chennai

- **Do you know him?**
  Yes, I know him.

- **Is he married?**
  Yes, he is married.

- **Is this your house?**
  Yes, this is my house.

- **How many rooms are there?**
  There are four rooms.

- **How long have you been here?**
  I have been here for six months.

- **Do you have any children?**
  Yes, I have two kids. A boy and a girl.

- **How old are they?**
  Arun is 16 and Sheela is 18

- **What does Sheela study?**
  She studies B.A., in American College

- **Do you have a computer?**
  No, I don't have

- **What time is dinner?**
  We dine around at 8 o'clock

- **Who cooks in your home?**
  My mother does the cooking .

- **Is your home near school?**
  No, it's far from here .

- **How often do you clean your room?**
  I clean daily.

- **Are you busy?**
  Yes, I am busy.

- **What animals do you like?**
  I like Elephant and Lion.

- **Where do your parents live?**
  My parents live in Mumbai

- **What did you buy?**
  I bought apple.

- **What did you say?**
  Nothing.

- **What time is it?**
  It's 10'o clock.

- **What is it?**
  It is a ball.

- **What is this?**
  This is a book.

- **What is that?**
  That is a clock.

- **What is his name?**
  His name is Sam

- **What day is it today?**
  Today is Friday

- **Where did you go?**
  I went to see my friends

- **Where do you want to go?**
  I want to go to the Temple

- **Whom did you meet?**
  I met my friends

- **When did you get home?**
  I arrived 10 minutes ago

- **Did you see him?**
  Yes, I saw him

- **What do you need?**
  I need water.

- **Do you want anything?**
  I don't want anything.

- **Do you want money?**
  Yes, I want money

- **How much do you want?**
  I want five thousand

- **Is this your book?**
  No, it is not my book

- **Are those yours?**
  Yes, those are mine

- **Do you understand?**
  No, I don't understand

- **How are you?**
  I am fine

- **How is your father?**
  He is fine

- **Are you hungry?**
  Yes, I am hungry

- **Are you serious?**
  Yes, I am serious

- **Where is my friend?**
  She is in the canteen

- **May I open the window?**
  Yes, you can

- **Can you swim?**
  No, I can't

- **What do you want to eat?**
  I want to eat Veg-Biriyani

- **Have you taken your breakfast?**
  Yes, I have taken my breakfast

- **Are you vegetarian?**
  No, I am not

- **What is your favourite book?**
  Harry potter

- **What is your favourite place to eat?**
  My favourite place is KFC

- **Which is your favourite movie?**
  My favourite movie is God Father

- **Who is your favourite Actor?**
  My favourite Actor is Tom Cruise

- **What is your favourite food?**
  My favourite food is Biryani

- **Are you staying alone?**
  No, I am staying with my friends

- **Are you busy?**
  Yes, I am busy with my work

- **Do you know swimming?**
  Yes, I know swimming

- **Does your school start at 8:00?**
  Yes, my school starts at 8:00.

- **Did you finish your homework?**
  Yes, I have finished my homework

- **Does your brother go to school?**
  Yes, my brother goes to school.

- **Did you make your bed?**
  Yes, I made my bed.

- **Did you go to bed early?**
  No, I didn't go to bed early.

- **Did you sleep well?**
  Yes, I slept well

- **Did you take a nap today?**
  No, I didn't take a nap.

- **Did you hear the sound?**
  No, I didn't hear anything

- **Did you invite him?**
  No, I didn't

- **Did you see anybody?**
  No, I didn't see anybody

- **Did he play well?**
  Yes, he played well

- **Did they eat anything?**
  Yes, they ate

- **Do you cook?**
  No, I don't

- **Do you remember me?**
  Sorry, I don't remember anything

- **Do you believe it?**
  No, I don't believe

- **Do you like music?**
  Yes, I like music

- **Do you want this book?**
  Yes, I want this book

- **Did you finish your drawing?**
  Yes, I finished my drawing.

- **Do you want vegetables?**
  Yes, I want

- **Do you want my help?**
  Yes, I want your help

- **How is your business?**
  It is going well

- **How many pencils do you have?**
  I have two pencils

- **Do you need anything?**
  No, thanks

- **Can you give me a hand?**
  No problem

- **Where can I get a taxi?**
  You can get it across the road

- **Is there a bank nearby?**
  Yes, there is

- **What is your phone number?**
  My phone number is 885061501

- **Could you please spell your name?**
  Yes, of course

- **Can you please say that again?**
  Yes, I say it again

- **Are you free tonight?**
  Yes, I am free tonight

- **Where did you go last night?**
  I went to the theatre

- **How was the movie?**
  Not, so bad

- **When does it begin?**
  It starts in the evening

- **Did you see this film?**
  Yes, I saw that film

- **Did you like the movie?**
  Yes, I like the movie

- **Did you enjoy?**
  Yes, I enjoyed

- **What is the story of the film?**
  The story is about an old man

- **Did you call me?**
  Yes, I called you

- **Did you get my message?**
  Yes, I got your message

- **Are you there?**
  Yes, I am

- **Are you happy?**
  Yes, I am happy

- **Could you do me a favour?**
  Yes, I am happy to help you

- **Could you finish your homework in an hour?**
  Yes, I could finish it in an hour.

- **Can you read this book?**
  Yes, I can read it.

- **Could you help me with my homework?**
  Yes, I could help you.

- **Could you speak English well?**
  No, I couldn't speak English.

- **What are you going to do today?**
  Today I am going to see a movie

- **Who is that boy?**
  He is my friend, Kevin

- **Who broke this?**
  I don't know

- **Why are you angry?**
  I fought with my friend

- **Can I try it on?**
  Sure, the trial rooms are over there

- **How much does it cost?**
  It's 500 rupees only

- **Can I pay by online?**
  Yes, you can

- **Do you have a car?**
  Yes, I have

- **What did you do?**
  I didn't do anything

- **What would you like tea or coffee?**
  I like coffee

- **What food do you like?**
  I like vegetable biryani

- **Could we have lunch together?**
  With pleasure

- **What is he like?**
  He is very friendly and helpful

- **Will you come to class tomorrow?**
  Yes, I will

- **Did you see anyone this week?**
  No, I didn't see anyone

- **What did you do this week?**
  I went to see my friends

- **Who is your best friend?**
  Vinoth is my best friend

- **Why do you lie?**
  No, I don't lie

- **Where does your dad work?**
  He works in a private company

- **Do you have any pets?**
  Yes, I have

- **Do you have any homework today?**
  Yes, I have lots of homework today

- **Did you do your homework?**
  Sorry, I forgot

- **Do you like to draw?**
  Yes, I like

- **What do you do when you get home from school?**
  I freshen up, drink coffee and eat snacks

- **Do you like to read?**
  Yes, I like

- **Did you write a letter?**
  Yes, I wrote a letter.

- **Did you help your sister with her homework?**
  Yes, I helped her.

- **Do you pray to God every day?**
  Yes, I pray

- **Does he study English?**
  Yes, he studies English.

- **Does your teacher speak English?**
  Yes, she speaks English.

- **Does your friend come to school by bus?**
  Yes, she comes by bus.

- **Are you going with him?**
  No, I am not

- **When will they come?**
  They will come at night

- **When do we leave?**
  We will go a little later

- **Won't you come?**
  No, I will not
- **Why are you tired?**
  Because of travelling
- **What are you doing here?**
  I am here to buy vegetables
- **Why are you shouting?**
  Because you are always playing mobile games
- **Why are you sad?**
  Because I have got bad marks in the exam
- **Why are you going to Mumbai?**
  I have an interview to attend
- **What is your address?**
  I stay at, 25 park town.
- **When and where were you born?**
  I was born in 2006 in Delhi
- **Where were you last week?**
  I was in Bangalore last week
- **May I open the window?**
  Certainly

- **Do you have any siblings?**
  Yes, I have a sister

- **What's your hurry?**
  I have an important work to do

- **Do you like my dress?**
  Yes, it's gorgeous

- **Can I turn on the TV?**
  No, it's time to study

- **Can you run?**
  No, I can't

- **May I take a rest?**
  Yes, you may

- **What did you learn today?**
  I learn English

- **Can you speak English?**
  No, I can't speak English.

- **Who is that person?**
  He is studying with me

- **How is the pain now?**
  The pain has gone now

- **Can you handle it?**
  Yes, I can handle it

- **What do you think?**
  I don't think about anything

- **What is on your mind?**
  I am just thinking

- **Can you answer this?**
  Yes, I know the answer

- **Can you help me with my homework?**
  Yes, I can help you.

- **Can you draw a picture of a cat?**
  Yes, I can draw a cat.

- **Who knows?**
  She knows about that

- **Am I wrong?**
  Yes, you are wrong

- **Do you think it is true?**
  I am afraid not

- **What did he say?**
  He said nothing

- **What does it mean?**
  I don't know

- **Where is she?**
  She has gone to the college

- **Who ate this?**
  She ate this

- **How many do you want?**
  I want five

- **Where can I sit?**
  Sit there

- **Is the toilet clean?**
  Yes, it is clean

- **Will it rain today?**
  It may rain today

- **Will she come?**
  Yes, she will come

- **Is it close to the railway station?**
  Yes, it is very close

- **Would you like to come with me?**
  Sure, I would love to

- **Do you know him?**
  Yes, I know him

- **What time do you close the shop?**
  I close at 10 a.m.

- **What time do you go to bed?**
  I go to bed at 10 p.m.

- **Why are you sad?**
  I have lost my book

- **Who took that?**
  I don't know

- **Is it your book?**
  Yes, it is mine

- **Can you find it?**
  Yes, I found it

- **Where is my phone?**
  Here, it is

- **When did you buy it?**
  I bought it yesterday

- **What is going on here?**
  They are fighting

- **Is she your sister?**
  Yes, she is my sister

- **How was your day?**
  It is fine

- **Can I eat this?**
  No, you can't

- **Who is next?**
  I am

- **Who goes first?**
  I go first

- **Shall I go?**
  Yes, you may go

- **Won't you go?**
  No, I will not go

- **Why are you crying?**
  My leg hurts

- **Can I help you?**
  No, thanks

- **Is he at home?**
  Yes, he is at home

- **Is anybody home?**
  Yes, who is it.

- **What are you talking about?**
  I am talking about Books

- **Who made it?**
  My mother made it

- **Who broke the vase?**
  I don't know

- **Can I put it there?**
  No, put it here

- **Did you see him go out?**
  Yes, I saw him

- **Has he arrived already?**
  Yes, he arrived in the morning

- **Will you join me for coffee?**
  Sorry, I have an important work

- **What is the temperature?**
  It is 40 degree Celsius now

- **What do you want to do tonight?**
  I would like to go to see a movie

- **What are you going to do tomorrow?**
  I am going to play football

- **What are you listening to?**
  I am listening to the music

- **What kind of music do you like?**
  I like melodious

- **Who is your favourite singer?**
  My favourite singer is Shreya Ghosal

- **What do you want to be?**
  I want to become an Engineer

- **What colour do you like?**
  I like Red

- **Have you seen Ram today?**
  No, he hasn't been around all day

- **Where did he go?**
  I don't know. Nobody knows

- **What is your favourite sport?**
  I like football

- **Who is your favourite team in IPL?**
  Chennai Super Kings

- **Do you know where this temple is?**
  Sure, it's over there

- **Is it far from here?**
  No, it's not far

- **How far is it?**
  About a half-kilo meter

- **Would you like to come with me?**
  Yes, let's go together

- **Do you know if there's a restroom around here?**
  Yes, it is across the street.

- **Do you know how to speak English?**
  Yes, I know

- **Where did you learn?**
  I learned by reading books

- **Do you like studying English?**
  Yes, I like studying English and I can read well.

- **Do you play with your friends after school?**
  Yes, I play with them.

- **Why do you study English?**
  I want to improve my English language

- **How long have you been studying English?**
  More than six years

- **How are you feeling?**
  I am all right

- **Where do you stay?**
  I am staying in Hotel

- **Is it a five-star hotel?**
  No, it is not

- **What is your profession?**
  I am a Teacher

- **What is going on here?**
  Nothing special

- **Are you happy?**
  Yes, I am happy

- **Do you like me?**
  Yes, I like you

- **What did you learn?**
  I learn many things

- **May I take a rest?**
  Yes, you may

- **Who is that person?**
  That person is my friend

- **May I sit next to you?**
  Yes, you can

- **Do you come tomorrow?**
  I will come if necessary

- **Can I switch on the fan?**
  Yes, you can

- **Do you need help?**
  Yes, thread the needle please

- **Can you please switch on the light?**
  Yes, I can

- **Can I write with a pen?**
  No, you cannot

- **Where is my pencil case?**
  Sorry, I don't know

- **Did you see my pencil case?**
  No, I didn't see it

- **Where do you want to go?**
  I want to go to the temple

- **Where did you go last weekend?**
  I went to the park last weekend

- **Do you like my new hairstyle?**
  No, it is different

- **Are you going to school today?**
  No, I am not well

- **Will you take a picture of us?**
  Yes, with pleasure

- **Would you like to play with me?**
  Yes, I would

- **Have you seen my keys anywhere?**
  No, I didn't

- **Did she tell you anything?**
  No, she didn't

- **Are you going to school by bus or by walk?**
  I am going to school by bus

- **When do you have school?**
  I have school from Monday to Friday.

- **When do you play outside?**
  I play outside after school, around 5 p.m.

- **When is your next holiday?**
  My next holiday is next week.

- **When do you start your homework?**
  I start my homework around 6 p.m.

- **Do you participate the competition?**
  No, I won't

- **Can you come with me?**
  Yes, I will

- **Have you had your lunch?**
  Yes, I had

- **How long have you been in Chennai?**
  Four years

- **Can I eat this?**
  No, it is rotten

- **Can you handle it?**
  Yes, I can handle it

- **Do you want a ride?**
  No, I don't

- **How is your cold?**
  It's fine

- **Is he a teacher?**
  Yes, he is a teacher

- **Is he still here?**
  Yes, he is here

- **Is it free?**
  No, it is not free

- **Is she at home?**
  No, she is not at home

- **Is he your brother?**
  Yes, he is my brother

- **Is that true?**
  No, that's not true

- **May I put it here?**
  Yes, you may

- **May I come in?**
  Yes, come in

- **Which one is real?**
  This one

- **When is school over?**
  At 4'o clock

- **Did you see anything?**
  No, I didn't

- **Did they find anything?**
  No, they didn't

- **Is anything broken?**
  No

- **How is it going?**
  It is going well

- **Do you need anything?**
  No thanks

- **Does air condition work?**
  No, it is not working

- **Do you drink water?**
  Yes, I drink water.

- **Is anybody here?**
  Yes

- **Do you like cooking?**
  Yes, I like cooking

- **Do I have to study?**
  Yes, you have to study for your future

- **Do you speak English?**
  I speak a little but not very well

- **Do you know that hotel?**
  Sorry, I don't know

- **What does your father do?**
  My father is a teacher.

- **Do you hear me?**
  Sorry, repeat again

- **Do you know us?**
  Yes, you are kamal's brother

- **Why do you ask?**
  Because he is a liar

- **Why do you lie?**
  No, I won't lie

- **Do you like music?**
  Yes, I love music

- **What do you need?**
  I need your help

- **Do you have a pet?**
  Yes, I love pets

- **Do you understand?**
  Yes, I understand

- **Do you want money?**
  Yes, I want to buy a book.

- **What does Vimal do?**
  He is a tailor.

- **When do you study?**
  I study early morning.

- **Do you play cricket?**
  Yes, I play cricket

- **Do you have a fever?**
  Yes, I have a fever of 102 degrees

- **Are you afraid of cockroach?**
  Yes, I am afraid of cockroach

- **Do you have a family?**
  Yes, I have a small family

- **Do you have blankets?**
  No, but I need a blanket

- **Do you think I am fat?**
  Not, too fat

- **What should I do now?**
  You should go to study now

- **Do you have any money?**
  No, I don't have

- **Do you need this book?**
  No, I don't need

- **Do you give to charity?**
  Yes, I love to donate

- **Do you want to be a business magnet?**
  Yes, of course

- **What do you want to do?**
  I want to earn a lot of money

- **What do you want to be?**
  I want to be a Teacher

- **Where do you have pain?**
  I have back pain

- **Will you do me a favour?**
  Of course

- **Will you go to the park today?**
  Yes, I will go to the park.

- **Will you help me with my homework?**
  Sure, I will help you.

- **Will you be my friend?**
  Yes, I will be your friend.

- **Will you clean your room?**
  Yes, I will clean it.

- **Will you play video games with me?**
  Yes, I will play with you.

- **Will you read a story before bed?**
  Yes, I will read a story.

- **Do you think I am stupid?**
  No, I don't think you are stupid at all

- **Do you have any brothers?**
  Yes, I have a brother and a sister

- **Do you have many friends?**
  Yes, I have many friends

- **Where do you work?**
  I work in an MRF Private Ltd.

- **What do you do on Sunday?**
  I play cricket on Sundays

- **Do you know who they are?**
  Yes, they are my relatives

- **What time do you go home?**
  I go home at 4 p.m.

- **Do you have a better idea?**
  Yes, I have

- **Do you know where he went?**
  No, I don't know

- **Do you have a pen?**
  Yes, of course

- **Do you like Chinese food?**
  No, I don't like it

- **What is your favourite colour?**
  My favourite colour is Red

- **Do you like sports?**
  Yes, I like sports

- **What is your favourite animal?**
  My favourite animal is Lion

- **What do you like to do in your free time?**
  I like to play with my friends

- **Do you have any brothers or sisters?**
  Yes, I have a sister

- **What is the weather like today?**
  It is cloudy

- **Do you like your school?**
  Yes, I like my school

- **Can you speak any other languages?**
  Yes, I can speak French

- **Do you like to read books?**
  Yes, I love reading books

- **What time do you wake up?**
  I wake up at 6 a.m.

- **What time do you go to bed?**
  I go to bed at 10 p.m.

- **What is your favourite TV show?**
  My favourite TV show is Super Singer

- **Can you ride a bicycle?**
  Yes, I can ride a bicycle

- **What is your favourite season?**
  My favourite season is summer

- **Do you have a pet?**
  Yes, I have a dog

- **What is your favourite game?**
  My favourite game is Chess

- **What is your best friend's name?**
  My best friend's name is Shreya

- **What do you want to be when you grow up?**
  I want to be an Artist

- **What is your favourite ice cream flavor?**
  My favourite ice cream flavor is vennila

- **Where is your school?**
  My school is in Anna Nagar

- **What is your favourite fruit?**
  My favourite fruit is mango

- **How do you get to school?**
  I go to school by walking

- **Do you play video games?**
  No, I don't play video games

- **Where were you born?**
  I was born in Chennai

- **Do you like animals?**
  No, I don't like animals

- **What is your favourite holiday?**
  My favourite holiday is Ooty

- **Do you like chocolate?**
  Yes, I like chocolate

- **Do you like to dance?**
  Yes, I like to dance

- **How many people are there in your family?**
  There are five people in my family

- **Do you like to go to the park?**
  Yes, I like going to the park

- **What do you want for your birthday?**
  I want storybook for my birthday

- **Do you like cooking?**
  Yes, I like cooking

- **What is your favourite flower?**
  My favourite flower is Rose

- **What is your favourite number?**
  My favourite number is 8

- **What do you do in the morning?**
  In the morning, I read newspaper

- **Whom do you live with?**
  I live with my grandparents

- **Do you have any cousins?**
  Yes, I have two cousins

- **What is your best friend like?**
  My best friend is like funny and kind

- **What do you do with your friends?**
  I play and talk with my friends

- **What is your mother's job?**
  My mother is an Auditor

- **Do you help your parents at home?**
  Yes, I help with cleaning and cooking

- **Do you live in a house or an apartment?**
  I live in an apartment

- **What time does school start?**
  School starts at 9 O'clock

- **What is your teacher's name?**
  My teacher's name is Sheela

- **Do you have homework?**
  Yes, I have Maths homework

- **Do you like Maths?**
  No, I don't like Maths

- **Do you wear uniform?**
  Yes, I wear uniform

- **What is the hardest subject for you?**
  The hardest subject for me is Science

- **Do you play an instrument?**
  Yes, I play the piano

- **Do you like drawing?**
  Yes, I like drawing

- **Do you collect anything?**
  No, I don't collect anything

- **Do you like watching movies?**
  Yes, I like watching movies

- **Do you like singing?**
  No, I don't like

- **Do you do any craft?**
  Yes, I like painting

- **What is your favourite outdoor activity?**
  My favourite outdoor activity is hiking

- **Do you like vegetables?**
  Yes, I like vegetables

- **What is your favourite restaurant?**
  My favourite restaurant is Taj Restaurant

- **Do you eat junk food?**
  No, I don't eat junk food

- **Do you like pizza?**
  No, I don't like pizza

- **Do you eat dessert?**
  Yes, I eat dessert

- **Have you ever been to another country?**
  No, I haven't been to another country

- **What is your favourite place to visit?**
  My favourite place is Kodaikanal

- **Do you like going to beach?**
  Yes, I love going to the beach

- **Do you prefer the city or the countryside?**
  I prefer countryside

- **How do you like to travel?**
  I like to travel by car

- **Do you like going to the zoo?**
  Yes, I like going to the zoo

- **What time do you go to school?**
  I go to school at 8 o'clock

- **What time does school finish?**
  School finishes at 4 o'clock

- **What do you do after school?**
  After school, I play with my friends

- **Do you take a nap in the afternoon?**
  Yes, I take a nap

- **What time do you have dinner?**
  We have dinner at 8 O'clock

- **Do you help with chores?**
  No, I don't help much

- **What time do you go to bed?**
  I go to bed at 9.30

- **How are you today?**
  I am tired

- **Are you feeling good today?**
  No, I don't feel good

- **Do you get angry easily?**
  No, I don't get angry easily

- **What do you do when you feel sad?**
  When I feel sad, I listen to music

- **Are you scared of anything?**
  No, I am not scared of anything

- **Do you like going for a walk?**
  Yes, I like going for a walk

- **Have you seen a rainbow before?**
  Yes, I have seen a rainbow

- **Do you like gardening?**
  Yes, I like gardening

- **Do you like camping?**
  No, I don't like camping

- **Do you have a phone?**
  Yes, I have a phone

- **Do you play games on your phone?**
  No, I don't play games on my phone

- **Do you watch videos on YouTube?**
  Yes, I watch cooking videos on YouTube

- **Do you use social media?**
  Yes, I use social media

- **What is your favourite app?**
  My favourite app is YouTube

- **Do you like technology?**
  Yes, I like technology

- **Do you know how to use a tablet?**
  Yes, I know how to use a tablet

- **How do you celebrate Christmas?**
  I celebrate by giving gifts, eating sweets etc.

- **Do you like Christmas?**
  Yes, I like Christmas

- **Do you exercise every day?**
  Yes, I exercise every day

- **Do you eat healthy food?**
  Yes, I eat healthy food only

- **Do you go to the gym?**
  Yes, I go to the gym

- **Do you drink enough water?**
  Yes, I drink enough water

- **Do you get carsick?**
  Yes, I get carsick sometimes

- **How many days are there in a week?**
  There are seven days in a week

- **What month is your birthday?**
  My birthday is in June

- **Do you like shopping?**
  Yes, I like shopping

- **Do you use credit cards?**
  No, I don't use credit cards

- **Do you have savings account?**
  Yes, I have savings account

- **Do you save money?**
  Yes, I save money

- **Do you buy clothes online?**
  No, I don't buy clothes online

- **Do you go to the mall often?**
  No, I go to the mall twice a week

- **Do you have many friends?**
  No, I don't have many friends

- **Do you spend a lot of time with your family?**
  Yes, I spend a lot of time with my family

- **What makes a good friend?**
  A good friend is loyal, trustworthy etc.

- **Do you like to share with others?**
  No, I don't share anything

- **What do you want to be when you grow up?**
  I want to be a teacher

- **What is your biggest goal in life?**
  My biggest goal is to become a billionaire

- **What subject do you find the easiest?**
  The easiest subject for me is English

- **What do you do with your family on weekends?**
  We have lunch together and play games

- **What is your favourite breakfast food?**
  My favourite breakfast food is Ven Pongal

- **What do you like to do in your free time?**
  I like to watch TV in my free time

- **How many rooms are there in your house?**
  There are four rooms in my house

- **What is your favourite cartoon?**
  My favourite cartoon is Tom and Jerry

- **Are you happy?**
  Yes, I am happy

- **Are you hungry?**
  No, I am not hungry.

- **Are you tired?**
  Yes, I am a little tired

- **Are you my friend?**
  Yes, I am your friend

- **Are you going to school?**
  Yes, I am going to school

- **Are we ready?**
  Yes, we are ready

- **Are they playing outside?**
  No, they are not playing outside

- **Are you tall?**
  No, I am not tall

- **Are we late?**
  Yes, we are a little late

- **Are your shoes new?**
  Yes, they are new

- **Are you scared?**
  No, I am not scared

- **Are the books on the table?**
  Yes, the books are on the table

- **Are you going home now?**
  Yes, I am going home now

- **Are you watching TV?**
  No, I am not watching TV

- **Are they your parents?**
  Yes, they are my parents

- **Are we in the right place?**
  Yes, we are in the right place

- **Are the flowers beautiful?**
  Yes, the flowers are very beautiful

- **Are you excited?**
  Yes, I am excited

- **Are you learning English?**
  Yes, I am learning English

- **Are the apples fresh?**
  Yes, the apples are fresh

- **Are we allowed to play now?**
  Yes, we are allowed to play now

- **Are you older than me?**
  No, I am younger than you

- **Are your parents at home?**
  Yes, my parents are at home

- **Are they your teachers?**
  Yes, they are my teachers

- **Are you from this town?**
  No, I am from another town

- **Are we going to the park?**
  Yes, we are going to the park

- **Are your friends coming over?**
  Yes, my friends are coming over

- **Are you feeling better?**
  Yes, I am feeling much better

- **Are there any bananas left?**
  No, there are no bananas left

- **Are we playing a game?**
  Yes, we are playing a game

- **Are you wearing a hat?**
  No, I am not wearing a hat

- **Are you reading a book?**
  Yes, I am reading a book

- **Are your friends here?**
  Yes, my friends are here

- **Are you going to bed now?**
  No, I am not going to bed yet

- **Are you good at drawing?**
  Yes, I am good at drawing

- **Are we all in the class?**
  Yes, we are all in the class.

- **Are you playing football?**
  Yes, I am playing football.

- **Are we having lunch now?**
  Yes, we are having lunch now.

- **Are you wearing glasses?**
  No, I am not wearing glasses.

- **Are they your pets?**
  Yes, they are my pets.

- **Are you working on a project?**
  Yes, I am working on a project.

- **Are you excited for the trip?**
  Yes, I am very excited for the trip.

- **Are you the oldest in your family?**
  No, I am the youngest in my family.

- **Are you practicing your piano?**
  Yes, I am practicing my piano.

- **Are we there yet?**
  No, we are not there yet.

- **Are you going to the party?**
  Yes, I am going to the party.

- **Are you ready for the test?**
  Yes, I am ready for the test.

- **Are we friends?**
  Yes, we are friends.

- **Whose toy is this?**
  This is my toy.

- **Whose book is on the table?**
  The book is mine.

- **Whose shoes are those?**
  Those are my brother's shoes.

- **Whose pencil is this?**
  It is Sheela's pencil.

- **Whose dog is barking outside?**
  The dog belongs to Smith.

- **Whose homework is this?**
  It's Sarah's homework.

- **Whose hat is on the chair?**
  It is my brother's hat.

- **Whose phone is ringing?**
  It's Dad's phone.

- **Whose bag is on the floor?**
  It's my bag.

- **Whose ball is in the yard?**
  The ball is mine.

- **Whose house are we visiting?**
  We are visiting Grandma's house.

- **Whose bike is outside?**
  It's my friend's bike.

- **Whose cup is on the counter?**
  It's Mom's cup.

- **Whose jacket is this?**
  It's my brother's jacket.

- **Whose car is parked in front of the house?**
  It's our neighbour's car.

- **Whose sunglasses are these?**
  They are my dad's sunglasses.

- **Whose candy did you eat?**
  I ate my candy.

- **Whose picture is on the wall?**
  It's a picture of my family.

- **Whose name is on the cake?**
  The name on the cake is Anushka

- **Whose shoes are in the hallway?**
  Those are Mom's shoes

- **Whose clock is on the wall?**
  It is my Grandma's clock

- **Whose birthday is today?**
  It's Kumar's birthday

- **Whose umbrella is this?**
  It's my cousin's umbrella.

- **Whose keys are on the table?**
  They are my dad's keys.

- **Whose room is this?**
  This is my room.

- **Whose glasses are on the shelf?**
  Those are my grandmother's glasses.

- **Whose bike did you borrow?**
  I borrowed Kevin's bike.

- **Whose pencil case is in the drawer?**
  It's my pencil case.

- **Whose birthday party are we going to?**
  We are going to Rachel's party.

- **Whose shoes are under the bed?**
  Those are mine.

- **Whose ball is that?**
  It's Deepak's ball.

- **Whose food is on the plate?**
  It's my food.

- **Whose ice cream did you eat?**
  I ate my own ice cream.

- **Whose chair is this?**
  It is my chair.

- **Whose sweater are you wearing?**
  I am wearing my sister's sweater.

- **Whose toys are scattered on the floor?**
  The toys are mine.

- **Whose painting is this?**
  It is my painting.

- **Whose shoes are in the outside?**
  Those are my brother's shoes.

- **Whose pen did you use?**
  I used my pen.

- **Whose lunch is in the fridge?**
  It's mine.

- **Whose towel is hanging in the bathroom?**
  It's Mom's towel.

- **Whose notebook is this?**
  It is Vimal's notebook.

- **Whose dog is that playing in the yard?**
  That's my friend's dog

- **Whose football is this?**
  It is Arun's football

- **Whose car is parked in the driveway?**
  It is my uncle's car

- **Whose birthday is coming up?**
  My brother's birthday is coming up

- **Why are you happy?**
  Because I got a new toy.

- **Why do you like school?**
  Because I love learning new things.

- **Why are you sad?**
  Because I lost my favourite pencil.

- **Why do we need to sleep?**
  To rest and feel better.

- **Why are you laughing?**
  Because I heard a funny joke.

- **Why is the sun hot?**
  Because it is a giant ball of fire.

- **Why do you eat vegetables?**
  Because they help me stay healthy.

- **Why do we brush our teeth?**
  To keep our teeth clean and strong.

- **Why do we need to drink water?**
  To stay hydrated and healthy.

- **Why do you go to school?**
  To learn new things and make friends.

- **Why do we wear clothes?**
  To keep warm and protect our bodies.

- **Why are you crying?**
  Because I am feeling upset.

- **Why do you like chocolate?**
  Because it tastes sweet and yummy.

- **Why is it cold outside?**
  Because it's winter.

- **Why do we celebrate birthdays?**
  To celebrate the day we were born.

- **Why do you wash your hands?**
  I wash my hands to remove dirt and germs.

- **Why do we have to exercise?**
  To keep our bodies strong and healthy.

- **Why do we need to be kind?**
  Because it makes everyone feel happy.

- **Why are you wearing a jacket?**
  Because it is cold outside.

- **Why do we need to wear shoes?**
  To protect our feet.

- **Why do you like your pet?**
  They are cute and fun to play with.

- **Why is it important to read?**
  Because reading helps us learn and grow.

- **Why do you go to bed early?**
  Because I need enough sleep to feel good.

- **Why do we need friends?**
  To have fun and help each other.

- **Why is your hair brown?**
  Because of the color of my hair genes.

- **Why do we need to follow rules?**
  To stay safe and be respectful.

- **Why do you like playing games?**
  Because it is fun and exciting.

- **Why do we need to go to the doctor?**
  To stay healthy and get better if we are sick.

- **Why do you sing songs?**
  Because it's fun and makes me happy.

- **Why is the traffic jam so long?**
  Because too many cars are on the road.

- **Why do we celebrate holidays?**
  To remember special events or traditions.

- **Why is the dog wagging its tail?**
  Because it is happy or excited.

- **When do you go to school?**
  I go to school at 8 a.m.

- **When do we eat lunch?**
  We eat lunch at 1o'clock

- **When is the movie starting?**
  The movie is starting at 3 o'clock.

- **When do you wake up on Sundays?**
  I wake up at 10 a.m. on Sundays

- **When do we play outside?**
  We play outside after school.

- **When is your next holiday?**
  My next holiday is in December.

- **When is the school bus coming?**
  The school bus is coming at 7.30 a.m.

- **When do you go to bed?**
  I go to bed at 9 p.m.

- **When is your cricket match?**
  My cricket match is on Saturday.

- **When do we leave for the trip?**
  We leave at 10 a.m. tomorrow.

- **When do you have piano lessons?**
  I have piano lessons on Mondays.

- **When is the party?**
  The party is on Sunday.

- **When does the rain stop?**
  The rain stops in the evening.

- **When is your friend coming over?**
  My friend is coming over at 4 p.m.

- **When does the school year start?**
  The school year starts in June.

- **When do you go shopping?**
  We go shopping on Saturdays.

- **When can we have ice cream?**
  We can have ice cream after dinner.

- **When are we going to the park?**
  We are going to the park this afternoon.

- **When does the sun set?**
  The sun sets at 6:30 p.m.

- **When does your favourite TV show start?**
  It starts at 7 p.m.

- **When is the next class?**
  The next class is in 10 minutes.

- **When do you feel happy?**
  I feel happy when I play with my friends.

- **When do we do our homework?**
  We do our homework after dinner.

- **When is the school field trip?**
  The school field trip is next Friday.

- **When do we visit Grandma?**
  We visit Grandma on Sundays.

- **When is the next test?**
  The next test is on Wednesday.

- **When do we have gym class?**
  We have gym class on Tuesdays.

- **When do you go to the swimming pool?**
  I go to the swimming pool in the summer holiday.

- **When do you wake up?**
  I wake up at 7 o'clock in the morning.

- **When do you go to bed?**
  I go to bed at 9 p.m.

- **When is your birthday?**
  My birthday is on July 15th.

- **When do you eat lunch?**
  I eat lunch at 12:30 p.m.

- **When do we leave for the trip?**
  We leave for the trip tomorrow morning.

- **When do you brush your teeth?**
  I brush my teeth in the morning and before bed.

- **When is your class?**
  My class is at 10 a.m. every day.

- **When does school end?**
  School ends at 3 p.m.

- **When do you have your break?**
  I have my break at 10:30 a.m.

- **When do we go to the park?**
  We go to the park in the afternoon, around 3 p.m.

- **When do you play with your friends?**
  I play with my friends after school and on weekends.

- **When does the bus arrive?**
  The bus arrives at 10 a.m.

- **When do we have dinner?**
  We have dinner at 8 p.m.

- **When do you feel happy?**
  I feel happy when I play with my friends.

- **When do you need help?**
  I need help when I don't understand my homework.

- **When do we celebrate Christmas?**
  We celebrate Christmas on December 25th.

- **When do you do your chores?**
  I do my chores on Sundays.

- **When does the movie start?**
  The movie starts at 2 p.m.

- **When do you need to wear a jacket?**
  I need to wear a jacket when it's cold outside.

- **When do you visit your grandparents?**
  I visit my grandparents every Sunday.

- **When do you go to the library?**
  I go to the library on Tuesdays after school.

- **When do you go swimming?**
  I go swimming in the summer when it is hot.

- **When does the school bus leave?**
  The school bus leaves at 7:00 a.m.

- **When is your next test?**
  My next test is on Friday.

- **When do you visit the park?**
  I visit the park on weekends.

- **When do we go to the park?**
  We go to the park in summer holidays.

- **When do you clean your room?**
  I clean my room every Sunday morning.

- **When do you feel sleepy?**
  I feel sleepy when I get tired.

- **When does school end?**
  School ends at 4 p.m.

- **When do you wear your uniform?**
  I wear my uniform on school days.

- **When is your school sports day?**
  Our sports day is on next month.

- **When do you read books?**
  I do my reading after dinner.

- **When do we go grocery shopping?**
  We go grocery shopping on Sundays.

- **When do you have music class?**
  I have music class on Saturday at 5 p.m.

- **When do you go to bed during the weekend?**
  I go to bed late on the weekend, around 11 p.m.

- **When is the best time to study?**
  The best time to study is in the morning.

- **When do you eat breakfast?**
  I eat breakfast at 8 a.m. before I go to school.

- **How do you feel today?**
  I feel happy today.

- **How is the weather?**
  The weather is sunny and warm.

- **How do you spell your name?**
  I spell my name S-h-e-e-l-a

- **How do you go to school?**
  I go to school by bus.

- **How many books do you have?**
  I have five books.

- **How can I help you?**
  You can help me by giving me the pencil.

- **How do you make a sandwich?**
  First, I put some bread then add cheese and vegetables.

- **How much does this toy cost?**
  It costs two hundred rupees.

- **How do you know her?**
  I know her from school.

- **How do you feel about the trip?**
  I am excited about the trip!

- **How long will it take to get there?**
  It will take about 30 minutes.

- **How do you play the piano?**
  I press the keys with my fingers.

- **How is the food?**
  The food is delicious!

- **How do you feel about your result?**
  I feel happy.

- **Where do you live?**
  I live in a small house near the park.

- **Where is the library?**
  The library is next to the playground.

- **Where is the bathroom?**
  The bathroom is down the hall, on the left.

- **Where are we going today?**
  We are going to the zoo to see the animals.

- **Where do you want to go for lunch?**
  I want to go to the pizza cut.

- **Where can I find my shoes?**
  Your shoes are near the door.

- **Where is your school?**
  My school is near the supermarket.

- **Where do birds sleep?**
  Birds sleep in the nests.

- **Where do we park the car?**
  We park the car in the parking lot behind the building.

- **Where do you keep your books?**
  I keep my books on the shelf in my room.

- **Where is your family from?**
  My family is from Chennai, but we live here now.

- **Where are my glasses?**
  Your glasses are on the table.

- **Where can I buy ice cream?**
  You can buy ice cream at the shop.

- **Where does the train go?**
  The train goes to Delhi.

- **Where is the park?**
  The park is down the street, near the big fountain.

- **Where are the keys?**
  The keys are on the kitchen counter.

- **Where is the nearest hospital?**
  The nearest hospital is just a few blocks away.

- **Where is your backpack?**
  My backpack is in the living room.

- **Where do you want to go on vacation?**
  I want to go to the beach and play in the sand.

- **Where is the ice cream shop?**
  The ice cream shop is next to the medical shop.

- **Where do you keep your toys?**
  I keep my toys in the toy chest in my room.

- **Where can I find the pencil?**
  The pencil is on the desk.

- **Where do you go for a swim?**
  I go to the private swimming pool.

- **Where did you go after school?**
  I went to the park with my friends to play cricket.

- **Where do you go to play?**
  I go to the playground to play with my friends.

- **Where are my socks?**
  Your socks are in the drawer, with your clothes.

- **Where is your favourite restaurant?**
  My favourite restaurant is on Main Street.

- **Where is the bakery?**
  The bakery is just down the road, next to the grocery store.

- **Where does the bus stop?**
  The bus stops right in front of the school.

- **Where do you keep your clothes?**
  I keep my clothes in the wardrobe, in my room.

- **Where are we having dinner tonight?**
  We are having dinner at Grandma's house.

- **Where is the nearest grocery store?**
  The nearest grocery store is two blocks away.

- **Where do you like to go shopping?**
  I like to go shopping at the mall.

- **Where does the airplane land?**
  The airplane lands at the airport on the runway.

- **Where do you keep your pencils?**
  I keep my pencils in the pencil case inside my bag.

- **Where is your brother?**
  He is in the garden, playing with his toy cars.

- **Where do you find the books you like to read?**
  I find books at the library.

- **Where did you go last weekend?**
  I went to the beach with my family.

- **Where do we go to get a haircut?**
  We go to the barbershop to get a haircut.

- **Where is the kitchen?**
  The kitchen is next to the dining room.

- **Where are your shoes?**
  My shoes are by the door, next to my coat.

- **Where do you like to go on weekends?**
  I like to go to the park and ride my bike with my friends.

- **Where is your favourite playground?**
  My favourite playground is in the park.

- **Where do you keep your schoolbooks?**
  I keep my schoolbooks in my desk at school.

- **Where can we find some toys?**
  You can find toys at the toy store from the supermarket.

- **Where is the classroom?**
  The classroom is on the second floor.

- **Where do we put our bags?**
  We put our bags in the lockers outside the classroom.

- **Where is the teacher?**
  The teacher is in the staff room right now.

- **Where can I find the whiteboard markers?**
  The whiteboard markers are in the drawer.

- **Where is the gym?**
  The gym is down the hall, past the library.

- **Where do we have lunch?**
  We have lunch in the canteen, next to the playground.

- **Where do we go for recess?**
  We go to the playground for recess.

- **Where is the principal's room?**
  The principal's room is on the first floor, near the entrance.

- **Where is the office room?**
  The office room is next to the principal's room.

- **Where is the library?**
  The library is on the ground floor, next to the computer lab.

- **Where do we put our homework note?**
  You can put your homework note on the teacher's desk.

- **Where do we go for the school assembly?**
  We go to the auditorium for the school assembly.

- **Where can I find my textbook?**
  You can find your textbook in the bookshelf.

- **Where do we keep our lunchboxes?**
  You can keep your lunchbox in the cupboard.

- **Where is the computer lab?**
  The computer lab is next to the art room, on the second floor.

- **Where can I find the stapler?**
  The stapler is in the drawer.

- **Where do we have our music class?**
  We have music class in the music room.

- **Where can I find the pencils?**
  The pencils are in the pencil holder.

- **Where is the school bus?**
  The school bus is parked at the backside of the school.

- **Where are we going for the field trip?**
  We are going to the science museum this Friday.

- **Where do we write our name on the assignment?**
  You write your name at the top of the paper, in the right corner.

- **Where is my backpack?**
  Your backpack is in the hallway, next to the coat rack.

- **Where do I store my coat?**
  You hang your coat on the hook in the hall.

- **Where is the television?**
  The television is in the living room.

- **Where are my shoes?**
  Your shoes are by the front door, near the shoe rack.

- **Where do you keep the cleaning supplies?**
  The cleaning supplies are under the kitchen sink.

- **Where can I find the scissors?**
  The scissors are in the drawer next to the kitchen counter.

- **Where is the phone charger?**
  The phone charger is in my room.

- **Where is the oven?**
The oven is in the kitchen.

- **Where is the bathroom?**
The bathroom is down the hall, on the left side.

- **Where is the refrigerator?**
The refrigerator is in the kitchen.

- **Where do you want to eat dinner?**
Let's eat dinner in the dining room tonight.

- **Where is the washing machine?**
The washing machine is in the laundry room.

- **Where do we keep the blankets?**
We keep the blankets in the closet.

- **Where is my pencil case?**
Your pencil case is on your desk in your room.

- **Where is the fruit bowl?**
The fruit bowl is on the kitchen table.

- **Where do you keep the medicine?**
I keep the medicine in the cabinet.

- **Where is the vacuum cleaner?**
The vacuum cleaner is in the closet near the front door.

- **Where is the clock?**
  The clock is on the wall.

- **Where is the dustbin?**
  The dustbin is in the kitchen, under the counter.

- **Where is the microwave?**
  The microwave is on the kitchen counter.

- **Where can I find a towel?**
  The towels are in the bathroom, near the sink.

- **Where do you keep the important documents?**
  I keep the important documents in the cupboard.

- **Where is your toy?**
  My toy is in the toy box in my room.

- **Where are my shoes?**
  Your shoes are by the front door.

- **Where do we keep the snacks?**
  The snacks are in the kitchen.

- **Where is the TV remote?**
  The TV remote is on the couch.

- **Where is your backpack?**
  My backpack is on the chair.

- **Where is the bathroom?**
  The bathroom is next to the kitchen.

- **Where is the kitchen?**
  The kitchen is next to the living room.

- **Where is my hat?**
  Your hat is on the shelf in the closet.

- **Where is the cat?**
  The cat is sleeping on the couch.

- **Where are the snacks?**
  The snacks are in the jar.

- **Where is your homework?**
  My homework is on the desk.

- **Where do you keep your toys?**
  I keep the toys in the living room.

- **Where is my pencil?**
  Your pencil is on the table, next to your notebook.

- **Where are the shoes?**
  The shoes are in the closet.

- **Where is your lunchbox?**
  My lunchbox is on the kitchen table.

- **Where is the dog?**
  The dog is in the kettle.

- **Where is the music player?**
  The music player is on the shelf in the living room.

- **Where is my water bottle?**
  Your water bottle is in the kitchen counter.

- **Where is the pencil sharpener?**
  The pencil sharpener is on my desk.

- **Where are the books?**
  The books are on the shelf in the living room.

- **Where is the ball?**
  The ball is in the backyard.

- **Where is the toothbrush?**
  The toothbrush is in the bathroom.

- **Where do you keep the keys?**
  I keep the keys on the key holder.

- **Where is your teddy bear?**
  My teddy bear is on my bed.

- **Where is the TV?**
  The TV is in the living room.

- **Where do you keep the towels?**
  The towels are in the bathroom.

- **Where is the torchlight?**
  The torchlight is in the drawer.

- **Where are the crayons?**
  The crayons are in the cupboard.

- **Where is the calendar?**
  The calendar is on the wall.

- **Where is my shirt?**
  Your shirt is hanging on the rack.

- **Where is the refrigerator?**
  The refrigerator is in the kitchen.

- **Where is the soap?**
  The soap is in the bathroom.

- **Where is the chair?**
  The chair is next to the table.

- **Where is the mirror?**
  The mirror is in the bathroom above the sink.

- **Where is the car?**
  The car is parked in the garage.

- **Where are your socks?**
  My socks are in the drawer.

- **Where is the window?**
  The window is next to my bed in my room.

- **Where are the cups?**
  The cups are in the cabinet above the sink.

- **Do you have many homework assignments?**
  No, I don't have many homework

- **Do you enjoy studying?**
  Yes, I enjoy studying

- **Do you have a favourite teacher?**
  Yes, my favourite teacher is Ramesh

- **Do you study in the morning or at night?**
  I study in the morning

- **Do you have a garden?**
  No, I don't have a garden

- **Do you live in a big house or a small house?**
  I live in a small house

- **Do you make your bed every day?**
  Yes, I make my bed every day

- **Do you visit relatives during the holidays?**
  Yes, I visit my relatives

- **Do you like nature?**
  Yes, I love nature

- **Do you like watching the stars?**
  Yes, I love watching the stars

- **Do you play sports?**
  Yes, I play football

- **Do you watch sports on TV?**
  Yes, I watch Tennis

- **Do you like reading books?**
  Yes, I love reading books

- **Do you watch cartoons?**
  Yes, I watch cartoons

- **Do you like rainy days?**
  No, I don't like rainy days

- **Do you like fast food?**
  No, I don't like fast food

- **Do you prefer tea or coffee?**
  I prefer coffee

- **Do you like spicy food?**
  No, I don't like spicy food

- **Do you wake up early?**
  Yes, I wake up early

- **Do you drink water in the morning?**
  Yes, I drink water in the morning

- **Do you exercise every morning?**
  Yes, I exercise every morning

- **Do you check your phone often?**
  No, I don't check my phone often

- **Do you go to bed early or late?**
  I go to bed early

- **Do you know how to cook?**
  Yes, I know how to cook

- **Do you eat out often?**
  No, I don't eat out often

- **Does she live in a big house?**
  Yes, she lives in a big house.

- **Does your mom like coffee?**
  No, she doesn't like coffee.

- **Does your mom cook dinner every day?**
  Yes, she cooks dinner every day.

- **Does she have a pet?**
  No, she doesn't have a pet.

- **Does your dad work on weekends?**
  No, he doesn't work on weekends.

- **Does she play the piano?**
  No, she doesn't play the piano.

- **Does your sister like to sing?**
  Yes, she likes to sing.

- **Does she like to dance?**
  Yes, she likes to dance.

- **Does she wear glasses?**
  No, she doesn't wear glasses.

- **Does she like ice cream?**
  Yes, she likes ice cream.

- **Does she go to the park after school?**
  Yes, she goes to the park.

- **Does she have a favourite colour?**
  Yes, she has a favourite colour.

- **Does your friend like chocolate?**
  Yes, she likes chocolate.

- **Does it rain often in your city?**
  Yes, it rains often.

- **Does your cat like to play with toys?**
  Yes, my cat likes to play with toys.

- **Does he have any brothers?**
  Yes, he has one brother.

- **Does he read books?**
  Yes, he reads books.

- **Does he play football?**
  Yes, he plays football.

- **Does he like playing video games?**
  Yes, he likes playing video games.

- **Does he watch cartoons?**
  Yes, he watches cartoons.

- **Does he know how to ride a bike?**
  Yes, he knows how to ride a bike.

- **Does he eat vegetables?**
  Yes, he eats vegetables.

- **Does your brother play video games?**
  Yes, he plays video games.

- **Does your family go on vacations?**
  Yes, my family goes on vacations.

- **Does your dog like to go for walks?**
  Yes, my dog loves going for walks.

- **Did you go to school today?**
  Yes, I went to school today.

- **Did you eat lunch?**
  Yes, I ate lunch.

- **Did you finish your homework?**
  No, I didn't finish my homework yet.

- **Did you play outside?**
  Yes, I played outside.

- **Did you watch TV yesterday?**
  No, I didn't watch TV yesterday.

- **Did you like the movie?**
  Yes, I liked the movie.

- **Did you visit the park last weekend?**
  Yes, I visited the park.

- **Did you read a book today?**
  Yes, I read a book.

- **Did you have breakfast this morning?**
  Yes, I had breakfast.

- **Did you call your friend?**
  No, I didn't call my friend.

- **Did you help your parents?**
  Yes, I helped my parents.

- **Did you enjoy the party?**
  Yes, I enjoyed the party.

- **Did you draw a picture?**
  Yes, I drew a picture.

- **Did you clean your room?**
  No, I didn't clean my room yet.

- **Did you learn something new today?**
  Yes, I learned something new.

- **Did you sing in the school play?**
  No, I didn't sing in the play.

- **Did you wear your new shoes?**
  Yes, I wore my new shoes.

- **Did you enjoy the music class?**
  Yes, I enjoyed the music class.

- **Did you make a new friend?**
  Yes, I made a new friend.

- **Did you see the rainbow?**
  Yes, I saw the rainbow.

- **Did you play a game with your brother?**
  No, I didn't play with my brother.

- **Did you ride your bicycle today?**
  Yes, I rode my bicycle.

- **Did you visit your grandparents?**
  No, I didn't visit them.

- **Did you bring your lunchbox?**
  Yes, I brought my lunchbox.

- **Did you make a cake?**
  No, I didn't make a cake.

- **Did you see your favourite animal at the zoo?**
  Yes, I saw my favourite animal.

- **Do you smoke?**
  No, I don't smoke

- **Did you buy new clothes?**
  No, I didn't buy any new clothes.

- **Did you meet your friends after school?**
  Yes, I met my friends.

- **Did you play with your pet today?**
  Yes, I played with my pet.

- **Did you see the stars last night?**
  Yes, I saw the stars.

- **Did you go swimming yesterday?**
  No, I didn't go swimming.

- **Did you clean your shoes?**
  Yes, I cleaned my shoes.

- **Did you play with toys today?**
  Yes, I played with my toys.

- **Did you get a good grade in school?**
  Yes, I got a good grade.

- **Did you learn how to ride a bike?**
  No, I didn't learn yet.

- **Did you enjoy the trip?**
  Yes, I enjoyed the trip.

- **Did you buy anything from the store?**
  Yes, I bought some candy.

- **Did you try a new food today?**
  Yes, I tried a new food.

- **Did you go on a school trip?**
  Yes, I went on a school trip.

- **Did you have fun today?**
  Yes, I had a lot of fun!

- **Did you see your teacher today?**
  Yes, I saw my teacher.

- **Did you play football after school?**
  No, I didn't play football.

- **Did you sing a song in music class?**
  Yes, I sang a song.

- **Did you get a present for your birthday?**
  Yes, I got a present.

- **Would you like some ice cream?**
  Yes, I would love some ice cream!

- **Would you like to play a game?**
  Yes, I would like to play a game.

- **Would you like to watch a movie?**
  Yes, I would love to watch a movie.

- **Would you eat vegetables if they were tasty?**
  Yes, I would eat them if they were tasty.

- **Would you like to visit the zoo?**
  Yes, I would like to visit the zoo.

- **Would you ride a horse if you could?**
  Yes, I would ride a horse.

- **Would you eat chappati for breakfast?**
  Yes, I would eat it for breakfast!

- **Would you like to learn how to swim?**
  Yes, I would like to learn how to swim.

- **Would you share your toys with your friends?**
  Yes, I would share my toys.

- **Would you read more books if you had time?**
  Yes, I would read more books.

- **Would you help me with my homework?**
  Yes, I would help you.

- **Would you help clean up after the birthday party?**
  Yes, I would help clean up.

- **Would you like to try a new sport?**
  Yes, I would like to try a new sport.

- **Would you play with your friends after school?**
  Yes, I would play with my friends.

- **Could you play the piano?**
  No, I couldn't play the piano.

- **Could you ride a bike when you were younger?**
  Yes, I could ride a bike when I was younger.

- **Could you finish the puzzle by yourself?**
  Yes, I could finish it by myself.

- **Could you sing a song for us?**
  Yes, I could sing a song.

- **Could you swim last summer?**
  Yes, I could swim last summer.

- **Could you eat the whole pizza?**
  No, I couldn't eat the whole pizza.

- **Could you ride a horse?**
  No, I couldn't ride a horse.

- **Could you read when you were in kindergarten?**
  No, I couldn't read back then.

- **Could you play football yesterday?**
  Yes, I could play football yesterday.

- **Could you draw a picture of a house?**
  Yes, I could draw a picture of a house.

- **Could you climb a tree when you were younger?**
  Yes, I could climb trees when I was younger.

- **Could you eat ice cream in winter?**
  Yes, I could eat ice cream in winter.

- **Could you run fast when you were in school?**
  Yes, I could run fast.

- **Could you play video games all day?**
  No, I couldn't play all day.

- **Could you ride a skateboard?**
  No, I couldn't ride a skateboard.

- **Can you ride a bike?**
  Yes, I can ride a bike.

- **Can you swim?**
  Yes, I can swim.

- **Can you sing?**
  Yes, I can sing.

- **Can you play Chess?**
  Yes, I can play Chess.

- **Can you play the piano?**
  No, I can't play the piano.

- **Can you jump high?**
  Yes, I can jump high.

- **Can you do a cartwheel?**
  No, I can't do a cartwheel.

- **Can you finish your homework by yourself?**
  Yes, I can finish it by myself.

- **Can you eat spicy food?**
  No, I can't eat spicy food.

- **Can you count 1 to 100?**
  Yes, I can count 1 to 100.

- **Can you run fast?**
  Yes, I can run fast.

- **Can you cook dinner?**
  No, I can't cook dinner yet.

- **Can you dance?**
  Yes, I can dance.

- **Can you ride a horse?**
  No, I can't ride a horse.

- **Can you make a paper boat?**
  Yes, I can make a paper boat.

- **Is your name Shreya?**
  Yes, my name is Shreya.

- **Is today your birthday?**
  No, today is not my birthday.

- **Is it raining today?**
  Yes, it is raining.

- **Is your favourite color blue?**
  Yes, my favourite color is blue.

- **Is school fun?**
  Yes, school is fun.

- **Is your pet a dog?**
  No, my pet is not a dog.

- **Is this your pencil?**
  Yes, this is my pencil.

- **Is it sunny outside?**
  Yes, it is sunny.

- **Is your friend coming to the party?**
  No, my friend is not coming.

- **Is your school near your home?**
  Yes, my school is near my home.

- **Is your brother older than you?**
  No, I am older.

- **Is there a library in your school?**
  Yes, there is a library

- **Is your house big?**
  No, my house is not big.

- **Is it cold outside?**
  Yes, it is cold.

- **Is your favourite subject Science?**
  Yes, my favourite subject is Science.

- **Is your dad at work?**
  Yes, my dad is at work.

- **Is it time for lunch?**
  Yes, it is time for lunch.

- **Is the sky cloudy?**
  No, the sky is clear.

- **Is your dog friendly?**
  Yes, my dog is friendly.

- **Is this your book?**
  No, this is not my book.

- **Is the movie good?**
  No, the movie is not good.

- **Is the movie about animals?**
  Yes, the movie is about animals.

- **Is there a park near your house?**
  No, there isn't a park.

- **Is your sister younger than you?**
  Yes, my sister is younger.

- **Is today a holiday?**
  Yes, today is a holiday.

- **Is your homework finished?**
  No, my homework is not yet finished.

- **Is there a supermarket near your house?**
  Yes, there is a supermarket near my house.

- **Is it a good idea?**
  Yes, it's a good idea.

- **Is your friend's birthday today?**
  Yes, it is my friend's birthday.

- **Is your mom at home?**
  No, my mom is not at home.

- **Is the cake ready?**
  Yes, the cake is ready.

- **Is it your turn to play?**
  Yes, it is my turn.

- **Is your teacher kind?**
  No, my teacher is not kind.

- **Is the food spicy?**
  Yes, the food is spicy.

- **Is an elephant big?**
  Yes, an elephant is big.

- **Is the ocean salty?**
  Yes, the ocean is salty.

- **Is a window made of glass?**
  Yes, a window is made of glass.

- **Is a tiger a wild animal?**
  Yes, a tiger is a wild animal.

- **Is chocolate sweet?**
  Yes, chocolate is sweet.

- **Is this your favourite song?**
  Yes, this is my favourite song.

- **Is it your first time here?**
  Yes, it is my first time.

- **Is this your first time here?**
  No, I've been here before.

- **Is your bike red?**
  No, my bike is not red.

- **Is the water cold?**
  Yes, the water is cold.

- **Is the bus coming soon?**
  Yes, the bus is coming soon.

- **Is your school big?**
  Yes, my school is very big.

- **Is the food ready to eat?**
  No, the food is not ready.

- **Is the sky blue?**
  Yes, the sky is blue.

- **Is a dog a pet?**
  Yes, a dog is a pet.

- **Is water wet?**
  Yes, water is wet.

- **Is the Earth round?**
  Yes, the Earth is round.

- **Is a cat smaller than a dog?**
  Yes, a cat is smaller than a dog.

- **Is ice cold?**
  Yes, ice is cold.

- **Is 5 bigger than 3?**
  Yes, 5 is bigger than 3.

- **Is a lion the king of the jungle?**
  Yes, a lion is the king of the jungle.

- **Is milk white?**
  Yes, milk is white.

- **Is a pencil used for writing?**
  Yes, a pencil is used for writing.

- **Is 3 plus 3 equal to 6?**
  Yes, 3 plus 3 is equal to 6.

- **Is it daytime now?**
  Yes, it's daytime now.

- **Is a banana yellow?**
  Yes, a banana is yellow.

- **Is a rabbit a mammal?**
  Yes, a rabbit is a mammal.

- **Was it your birthday yesterday?**
  Yes, it was my birthday yesterday!

- **Was she at school this morning?**
  No, she wasn't at school this morning.

- **Was the movie good?**
  Yes, the movie was good.

- **Was he tired after the game?**
  Yes, he was very tired after the game.

- **Was your mom happy with your result?**
  No, she wasn't happy with my result.

- **Was it raining when you went outside?**
  No, it wasn't raining when I went outside.

- **Was the classroom clean yesterday?**
  Yes, the classroom was clean yesterday.

- **Was the test difficult?**
  Yes, the test was very difficult.

- **Was she excited for the trip?**
  Yes, she was very excited for the trip.

- **Was the book interesting?**
  Yes, the book was interesting.

- **Was he scared of the dark?**
  No, he wasn't scared of the dark.

- **Was the park crowded on Sunday?**
  Yes, the park was crowded on Sunday.

- **Was she feeling sick yesterday?**
  Yes, she was feeling sick yesterday.

- **Was the food spicy?**
  No, the food wasn't spicy.

- **Were you at school yesterday?**
  Yes, I was at school yesterday.

- **Were they happy with the surprise?**
  Yes, they were happy with the surprise.

- **Were the students in class this morning?**
  Yes, the students were in class this morning.

- **Were you playing outside this morning?**
  No, I wasn't playing outside this morning.

- **Were the teachers strict yesterday?**
  No, the teachers weren't strict yesterday.

- **Were you tired after the walk?**
  Yes, I was tired after the walk.

- **Were the books on the table?**
  Yes, the books were on the table.

- **Were they at the park when you went?**
  No, they weren't at the park when I went.

- **Were the children excited for the game?**
  Yes, the children were excited for the game.

- **Were they waiting for the bus?**
  Yes, they were waiting for the bus.

- **Were you with your family last weekend?**
  Yes, I was with my family last weekend.

- **Were the flowers in the garden beautiful?**
  Yes, the flowers were beautiful.

- **Were you playing video games yesterday?**
  No, I wasn't playing video games yesterday.

- **Were you listening to music?**
  Yes, I was listening to music.

- **Were the lights on in the house?**
  Yes, the lights were on in the house.

- **Were you at home last night?**
  Yes, I was at home last night.

www.ingramcontent.com/pod-product-compliance
Ingram Content Group UK Ltd.
Pitfield, Milton Keynes, MK11 3LW, UK
UKHW021409190726
13845UKWH00028B/968

9 788196 496128